JOURNEY

TOWARD

THE

ROOTS

Valkyrie
Press, Inc.

811. 54
J93j
103531
Jan. 1978

Published By

Valkyrie
Press, Inc.

2135 1ST AVENUE SOUTH
ST. PETERSBURG, FLORIDA 33712

"... *Our past is not behind us, it is in us. Not as blank parchment or dead clay, shapeless and without form, do we march onward to our future, nor with empty hands. We bring to posterity the gift of a great and ancient heritage.*"

Ben-Gurion in
"The Call of the Spirit,"
the Israel Year Book, 1951

———————

Again, for Ilse

Other Books by the Author:

Hebraic Modes, Olivant Press, 1972.

From the Divide, Olivant Press, Homestead, Fla., Hardcover, 1st Ed., March, 1970; 2nd Paperback Ed. Dec. 1970; 3rd & 4th editions, Library Bound, Mar. & April, 1972.

Sermons from the Ammunition Hatch of the Ship of Fools, Vagabond Press, New Orleans, 1968, with a grant from the National Foundation for the Arts.

Florida Montage, South and West, Inc., 1966.

Existential Canon, South and West, Inc., Ft. Smith, Arkansas, 1965.

In Need for Names, Linden Press, Baltimore, Md., 1961.

I Feed You From My Cup, Quinnipiac College, Hamden, Conn., 1958.

ACKNOWLEDGMENTS

Passage from Ben-Gurion taken from *Ben-Gurion,* by Robert St. John, Doubleday & Co., Inc., Garden City, N.Y., 1971.

Six poems selected from *Omnibus,* University of South Florida.

Several poems selected from *South and West,* from *Hebraic Modes,* Olivant Press, and from the *South Florida Poetry Review.*

Sketches by the Author

JOURNEY

TOWARD

THE

ROOTS

A COLLECTION OF POEMS

BY

HANS JUERGENSEN

WITH AN INTRODUCTION BY ELIE WIESEL

INTRODUCTION
(Translation)

I have not yet met Hans Juergensen, but I believe I know him: he is a poet who sings about the not-quite-real life of a certain Moses Rosenberg. And this Moses Rosenberg is *himself.* That seems complicated, I realize; however, it is not, for in poetry all is simple — or ought to be, since poetic language may appear obscure without actually being so. It is a question of acceptance and understanding.

Let us explain: son of Esther Rosenberg, the poet was adopted by Hermann and Dora Juergensen. Born in Myslowitz — not far from Auschwitz — he grew up in metropolitan Berlin and provincial Schwiebus. What follows, you can imagine: tauntings, ridicule, persecution and, finally, escape abroad. Shattered again and again, his existence was made up of many new beginnings. He moved from family to family; from school to school; from Berlin to Newark — a stranger everywhere, yet everywhere at home. He loved those who sheltered him; he accepted each refuge — even welcomed the army which sent him first to North Africa, and then to Anzio via Monte Cassino. It is the poet in him who responds to every event. He lives in order to sing; he sings in order to bear testimony.

The poets are the great *witnesses* to this era. More than the scholars, better than the novelists, they testify for history. Indeed, I will go further and submit that it is they who are the true historians of their generation — a stammered verse, the fragment of a poem often communicate — on the most human level — a time of fear, a moment of death. Paul Celan, Nelly Sachs and the children of Terezin express in their poetry the human condition and destiny far more effectively than do the subsequent treatises of specialists.

I know: Hans Juergensen, like Nelly Sachs and Paul Celan, did not go through the crucible of the concentration camps; rather, he felt the fires from afar. But Moses Rosenberg (his alter ego) was there. Hence the power in certain of these songs. One cannot read them without emotion; for the poet speaks of the loneliness, the memory, the quest of the Jew. And we hear the somber invocations of Moses Rosenberg — that voice which was to survive in Hans Juergensen.

This voice, then, echoes the former; yet its tone has changed: it sounds more open, more cosmopolitan as it were; and, surely, more varied — embracing Pablo Neruda and Mozart, Kafka and Pablo Casals; reminiscences from journeys as well as imaginery encounters; and the visions lived by the wanderer who forever searches for something, or someone, that remains forever elusive, but elicits exclamations of joy or subdued anguish from the pilgrim standing on his ancient soil . . . reflections and inquiries from a teacher who instills his fervor into his young and disoriented students.

But it now comes to pass that these two voices are fused into one, grave and disquiet, which we at length apprehend for the enrichment of our own.

Elie Wiesel
New York — March 1976

INTRODUCTION

Je n'ai jamais recontré Hans Juergensen mais je crois le connaitre: c'est un poète qui chante la vie non-vècue d'un certain Moses Rosenberg. Et Moses Rosenberg c'est lui. Cela semble compliqué, je sais; ça ne l'est pas. En poésie tout est simple — ou devrait l'ëtre. Le langage poétique peut paraitre obscur sans ëtre compliqué pour autant. Il s'agit de l'accepter — de l'adopter.

Expliquons-nous: fils d'Esther Rosenberg, le poète a été adopté par Hermann et Dora Juergensen. Né à Myslowitz —non loin d'Auschwitz — il grandit à Berlin. La suite, vous l'imaginez: brimades, persécutions, fuite à l'étranger. Mille fois brisée, son existence est faite de commencements et plus encore de recommencements. Il va de famille en famille, de lycée en lycée, de Berlin à Newark, étranger partout et en même temps chez lui partout: il aime tous ses parents adoptifs, tous se refuges; il aime même l'armée qui l'envoie en Afrique du Nord, puis à Anzio via Monte-Casino. C'est le poète en lui qui aime tout ce qui lui arrive; il vit pour chanter, il chante pour témoigner.

Les poètes sont les grands témoins de ce temps. Plus que les savants, plus que les romanciers, ce sont eux qui déposent pour l'histoire. J'irais même plus loin et je dirai que ce sont eux les vrais historiens de leur génération. Un vers brisé, un fragment de poème communiquent parfois, à l'échelle humaine, ce que fut le temps de la peur, le temps de la mort. Paul Celan, Nelly Sachs, les poèmes des enfants de Terezin en disent plus sur la condition et le destin des hommes que les ouvrages spécialisés que la question.

Je sais: Hans Juergensen, comme Nelly Sachs et Paul Celan, n'a pas vécu l'événement — ou plutôt il l'a vécu de loin. Mais Moses Rosenberg l'a vécu. D'où la force de certains de ses chants. On ne peut les lire sans émotion. Il parle de la solitude juive, de la mémoire juive, de la quête juive et nois entendons la voix mélancolique de Moses Rosenberg, le survivant que Hans Juergensen aurait pu devenir.

La voix de Hans Juergensen, elle, ressemble à la première mais son registre est différent. Plus ouvert, plus cosmopolite pour ainsi dire. Plus varié surtout. Pablo Neruda et Mozart, Kafka et Pablo Casals. Souvenirs de voyage, rencontres imaginaires, rêves vécus d'un errant à la recherche de quelque chose ou de quelqu'un d'insaisissable; cris de joie ou d'angoisse étouffés d'un pélerin se retrouvant sur sa terre ancienne; reflexions et interrogations d'un professeur communiquant sa ferveur à ses étudiants encore jeunes, déroutés.

Mais il arrive que ces deux voix se rejoignent et alors un chant, grave et inquiétant, nous emporte au loin enrichir le nôtre.

Elie Wiesel
New York, Mardi 1976

GLOSSARY

Readers who have visited Israel will readily recognize place names and historical allusions in this collection.

For those not yet familiar with the land — sacred to Jews, Christians and Moslems — the author has taken the liberty of supplying a brief data so that footnotes may be avoided.

1. MORIAH:

a. The mountain on whose peak Abraham offered Isaak (Yitzhak) as sacrifice;

b. where Solomon built the first Temple, ca. 922 B.C.;

c. whence Mohammed ascended to heaven for one night — thus the rock enshrined in the "Dome of the Rock," completed 691 C.E.

2. YAD VASHEM: *

"Tent of Remembrance " the beautifully simple, stark memorial to the six million victims of the Holocaust. Its floor exhibits plaques naming the extermination camps. * Literally: "Hand of the Name."

The avenue of the "Trees of the Just" commemorates Gentiles who saved Jews from the Nazis.

3. THE SHRINE OF THE BOOK:

The structure which houses the Dead Sea Scrolls and the Bar Kochba letters; Bar Kochba led the last Jewish revolt against the Romans between 132 and 135 C.E.

4. DENMARK SQUARE MONUMENT:

An abstract iron sculpture, symbolizing a boat as used by the Danes to smuggle Jews to safety.

5. DAVID'S CITADEL:

Actually Herod's, and later a crusader, fortress. David conquered the Jebusite city in 1000 B.C.

6. MT. SCOPUS:

From the Greek "skopeo," to watch; the ridge northeast of Jerusalem where the original Hadassah Hospital and Hebrew University are located. From 1948 to 1967, a small Israeli garrison occupied the site, while Jordanians surrounded their position. The Israeli soldiers were relieved by airlift every two weeks.

7. THE GOLDEN GATE:

The gate through which Jesus entered Jerusalem, and which will receive the Messiah on the Day of the Last Judgment.

8. MEA SHEARIM:

"A hundred Gateways " the orthodox Jewish enclave, built 1875 by European Jews, outside the Old City.

9. GILEAD:

Pronounced Gilad. The mountain range east of the Jordan River.

10. YESHIVA BOCHER:

A student at an orthodox school or college.

11. MAOS HAYYIM:

A Kibbutz on the Jordanian border, southeast of Bet Shean.

12. BELVOIR — "BEAUTIFUL VIEW":

Crusader Castle overlooking the Jordan Valley, Mt. Tabor and the Galilee. It was besieged by Sultan Saladin (Salah-ed-din), died 1193, and later totally destroyed.

13. ROSH HA-NIQRA:

Chalk and limestone cliffs on the Mediterranean coast, bordering directly on Lebanon. The sea has created grottos and pools here which can be visited by means of tunnels.

14. THE CHAGALL WINDOWS:

These twelve stained glass windows, representing Israel's tribes, were designed by Marc Chagall for the chapel of the New Hadassah Hospital.

PILGRIMAGE

Journey toward the roots
of centuried holiness

where voluptuous groves
deny recorded deserts
and wadis again
stretch harvest carpets

where high reliefs
of alabaster towns
thrust defiant shadows
at hostile ranges

exclamation-marked
by minaret fingers
belfry spikes
and refurbished arks

where young conglomerates
crowd wired borders
— vibrant as bazaars —
from Dan to Barsheeba

. . . not yet at peace
but feverishly sanguine
in the creation
of new forevers

JERUSALEM

God's ineffable will
has swept history
within its golden walls.

The ramparts stand mighty,
but they were breached
by countless nations.

Each stone has been bled.

Still, the magnet of Moriah
draws streams of descendants
to replenish remembrance

and faith.

SYMBIOSIS
(The Dome of the Rock)

Unshod,
I circled the cream facets
of the Rock,
its myth-riven peak —
and recalled
Yitzhak's passion
and Mohammed's triumph.

Here, the Ark reposed,
unveiled once yearly
by the contriteness
of the high priest's palms.

Close by,
Jeshua confounded
rabbinic sagacity
before reaching
his ritual manhood . . .

The carpets stretched
in Persian silence.
Dusky gold seeped
through the oriental geometry
of gemmed glass

                    down

upon the very fulcrum
of my One-God universe.

the WALL
— aleph —

that colossal whiteness

pitted by millenia
of yearning contact

block
heaped
upon block —
the *specious* foundation
of Solomon's glory
and Herod's concession
to a sceptical Judah

lost
regained —
always through
youthful immolation

moss stippled

where even the
Assimilated
choke up
when exposed
to the keening
of obdurate believers

the WALL

— beth —

gravely
my handtips graze
those gritty seams
of the Wall
beseeching every
lip-served rill
recording ancestry

dismembered
like golden cherubim
on acacia ark
shredded like scrolls
salvaged from subjugation
braided into
my people's skin
sealed in its cause:

to outlast
exodus forevers

Yad Vashem

we *had* to enter

our veins ice-burned
with trepidation
our brains sparking
terror bursts

from sun to gehenna
a hesitance of step
past the burgeoning Trees
of the Just

walls meeting roof
in a tabernacle
portals a somberness
of sculpted splinters

our heart beats
slowly tolled us

inside

• • •

six million minute squares
like random bits of coal
totally huge

a world's soul
consumed
by inlaid letters:
      Majdanek
      Auschwitz
      Belsen-Bergen

this mosaic of anguish
encased
in that stark cube
of naked stone-heads

toward which
we turn
to touch the name-echoes
that flicker
through the mystic fingers
of eternal flame

SHRINE OF THE BOOK

one must pass
underground
first
before issuing into
the suffusion of clarity

. . . moving as in a trance
wrapped in a giant Torah
immured within traditions
of tacked-up
faded fibers
long sealed from history —
though undyingly
transmitted
by substance-of-mouth

        Bar Kochba's missives
        (triple-tongued)
        haggling for supplies

        the Dead Sea scrolls
        (re-puzzled)
        confirming messianic missions . . .

one presses close
against dividing panes
and knows
        for once
where one belongs

THE DENMARK SQUARE MONUMENT
IN JERUSALEM

Blessed those small,
unlighted vessels
which smuggled the condemned
out of the executioner's reach.

More blessed still
their crews,
compassionately scornful
of the master race.

Most blessed the nation
that sewed yellow stars
upon its sleeves
to face down swastikas.

They were indomitable.

And when I stood
before the symbol-ship —
iron as Danish courage —
I thought of my father

Who was a gentle branch
of that glorious tree.

Henry Moore

Billy Rose Sculpture Garden
Jerusalem
Aug 21, '74

FIGURES
(Henry Moore)

Out of earth's muscle
the compacted block
wrenched from some mountain wound
its raw sienna ribbed to his awed palm
he made his contribution:

balanced the planes
for onyx instants
melding into gray rose
and green pores
toward umber
where shadows mark the modeling

rounded all sharpnesses away
for the continuum
of the sight's embrace
softly solid
unchanging though constantly altered
in the viewing

the thinking around
the attempting to peel off
correspondence to one's own
image
reversely fashioned

. . . to carve a pose of thought
so intricately simple
so harmony-implied
forces meretricious time
to hold its breath this once
for man to claim it his

The Citadel
Jerusalem

DAVID'S CITADEL

through his still shepherd instincts
he unearthed
the Jebusite life-line
and
with a handful of swords
clambered up its conduit
into the innermost defenses

now
the summit was his
to designate it —
fervently —
City of Peace . . .

though not without embrasures
nor proper fields of fire
newly engineered
upon already hoary bastions

— thus to evolve
as the vortex
of dogma-fingered conquests
forever diminished
or added unto

fanatically sullied
by rival Armageddons

REFLECTIONS ATOP
MT. SCOPUS

If the Lord God
at any date descended
for a close-up
of His stiffnecked servants,
He undoubtedly hovered
above *this* sentry-spur
of Zion,
from whose flanks
so many scions
of contentious tribes
burst southward
beyond Nehemiah's wall.

His omnipotence
would also have beheld
the sunrise wilderness —
an arid buckling of His earth —
around that saline sea
which He had once commanded
to drown out sin . . . forever!

Perhaps, He —
Who sleeps nor slumbers not —
will give the present
some undivided concentration
and place a calm
on all the armored claimants
of His hills.

THE GOLDEN GATE

Suleiman,
having re-walled
the earth's focus,
bricked up this thoroughfare;

uneasily, to be sure,
but solidly
since venerable sources —
both Talmudic
and Nazarene —
presaged
the Messiah's penetration
through just that arch.

The Magnificent Sultan,
however humanistically
enlightened,
could not take chances
on those odds . . .

CHURCH OF THE NATIVITY

At the foot of raw steps
the daggers of the star
stab my sight.

Tapers flick
shadows
against one another.

. . . Here was
born
the Child.

Dankness constricts
the manger
with foreboding.

Its sanctity dims
the consciousness
of joy.

ENCOUNTER

Descending from Judea's hills
he ruffled his beard
with defiant fingers
and smoothed the
temptation-saturated robe.

i ascended from the valleys.

and we met.

"shalom" he saluted.
"shalom" i replied.

"are you one of my people?"

"i don't know.
your people have made matters
difficult for mine
since you acquired
those perforations."

his mouth tautened:
"they are not my people!"

no. they really are not.

he and i shared the longing
of Israel's eyes —
both fishermen
with words for nets.

we might have become friends
despite the centuries
that made him into god
and me into ashes . . .

MEA SHEARIM

My sandals tap
about the un-reformed fortress
of a "Hundred Gates",
through the bustling narrowness
between antique stalls;

manned by black gabardine
with silken beards
and studied curls,
roofed by felt brims
or fur perimeters;

interspersed with reticent women,
lawfully dowdy —
though proud as matriarchs
and vocal, scurrying copies
of fundamental elders.

— I am of their blood, too,
yet a stranger
to this introverted enclave
which disdains
my world of time
and obstinately bends
over its five
unalterable scrolls . . .

JOURNEY ON THE WEST BANK

Rock 'n Roll pelted the passengers;
so did a dry sun,
as our bus negotiated
the Jericho road,
tooling along beige barrenness.

There was little to say;
but tourists began
to comprehend
Joshua's tactical intuition,
for the slopes were punctuated
by redoubts —
their weaponry today's,
their placement
the Old Testament's.

To the east
rose Gilead's spine,
at whose base
clumps of cypress marked
the course of the holy river
which separates insecure cousins.

. . . a Yeshiva Bocher flipped
the leaves of his Midrash,
quite oblivious
to all that bitter history.

Bomb proof
Maotz Haim,
aug 24.

KIBBUTZ

Olive trees gnarl haughty trunks
up into August crowns,
their harvest yet unborn.

Spaced between them —
like ungainly dromedary humps —
loom bomb proofs,
grim as repeated threats
issuing from chalked-up jaws.

But — splashed along concrete,
hang the expressionist explosions
caused by Van Gogh, Matisse
plus other beautifiers.

And very new Sabras
chase one another
about those
not always idle caves.

Belvoir Castle
12th Century
Hospitaller Knig
aug 86

#94

38

CRUSADER CASTLE

Hard by the west gate's
proto-gothic vault
the pilgrim will discover
Seraphim
carved upon native marble —
their ancient guardianship
transposed
from Yahve's tabernacle
to Hospitaller ward.

Other pure Hebraic relics
still trim
diverse ramparts
of martial masonry.

The minions of St. John —
having run short
of Christian boulders —
had to make do
with Jewish substitutes,
hoping to cancel out
Mosaic potencies
by the incising
of spiked crosses
at strategic points.

However,
well-disposed batteries
of Salah-ed-din's
mangonels
took weighty exception
to such dichotomies
and soon reduced
the 'Bel-Voir'
to heaps of infidel rubble.

THE JORDAN NEAR
MAOS HAYYIM

Potentials of death
parallel tacky macadam,
their detonator pins piercing
cracked clay.

Behind this brutal margin
a lush slope screens
the scriptural river;
and I must leap a mine
for the view
where the intensity
of regal blue
uncoils a mere twenty paces
of legendary breadth,
set off by Gilead ochre.

. . . turning south,
I stand dazzled
by the white grace
of the "Doves' Cliff",
mounted like a temple —
while, from the north,
an olive drab command car
field-glasses
my possible intentions . . .

צבי
ישי

Aug 25, 74
Kibbutz Ha'oz Haim

42

YITZHAK ZWI
(a portrait)

He fidgeted
when I bade him pose
for my selfish pen.

I cajoled: "Es nimmt nischt keen Zeit."

He relaxed a bit;
but his head —
that experienced rock,
sturdily set upon
the horizontal
of his hirsute shoulders —
turned quizzically
toward his wife;

A shadow-grin
creasing his lips,
edging embarrassment.

Yet, his eyes —
their hibiscus crinkles
spreading to the temples —
cupped pioneer sparks
and — finally —
mirrored mine.

My pen struck swiftly
and caught his life force
like a Halleluiah!

Beggar in Haifa

Into the eddy
of five o'clock transients
shuffled a beggar,
deliberate as a zadik,
offering his cup
to each member
of the populace.

About to drop
a pittance
into his tin,
I gave him
a second glance
and — meeting
a smug countenance —
desisted . . .

IN A YEMENITE WORKSHOP

With a most delicate mallet
he pinged filigree prayers
into the yielding silver
of an emerging Menorah.

His spectacles slid down
the ancient ridge of nose
so that astute eyes
might verify the glow
of my admiration
or the lace of his design.

And the solemnity of his beard
could not conceal
the beatific smile
of a devout
but self-reliant master.

REUNION IN TEL AVIV
— AUG., 1974

I still see myself,
barely coming up to his belt,
at our last encounter
on a Berlin platform.

He had just pulled me
out of a 3rd class window
with his Maccabi bravado
while I clutched
at his hair.

Today,
forty-five years older,
our eyes existed
on a perfect level —
our skulls not yet deforested
though timed by snow.

The talk leaped through hoops
of mutual interruptions —
all those decades
neatly peeled off . . .

We liked each other

and celebrated our *Wiedersehen*
over platters
of garnished mullets
in a Turkish establishment.

for Max Grossmann

ROSH HA-NIQRA

Aeons attacked the cliffs
clawing breath-catching pools
into chalk and lime

Hard-pressed fugitives
spun subterranean nets
as a last retreat
for the dispossessed —

Sea fists churn up
a compressed
vengeful surf
whose pounding stills
all other voices

Cunningly shifting greens
peak in surrealist waves
under the purple
of reverberating ceilings

Each cavern lip
gleams blinding white

           I walk this underworld
           clutched by a
           strangely *neutral* awe

THE CHAGALL WINDOWS

o the fires!
       orange fierceness
       crimson bloom

o the seas!
       beryl surf
       cobalt foam

o the creatures!
       wingéd
       horn-tipped
       multi-hued
       like Joseph's robes

o the yield of Canaan!
       strewn across
       the glass expanse
       of jewelled tribes

o the light upon our souls!
       born of sun
       and genius

o the AMEN to our kind!

PSALM

Let the chant of your pulse
count the stalks
of your brethren
and your blood will name
each being.

Whatever IS
is bound to your eyes
to dwell in your seeking
from day to day.

For the skein of the word
threads endless:
You weave it of song
or of sorrow —
each in its course.

And no one may taste
honey only
nor bitterroot.

Seasons must alter
the truths of the valleys —
Then
like an arbor
shall Israel flourish!

EREF YOM KIPPUR

Under the renewed moon
the hills of Judea gleam
linen-robed like the Law
whose snow-austerity
is hemmed with threads
of golden homage. —

Before the Ark,
the appointed one
intones humility
as the first supplicant
this night,
to be adjudged
by the weight of his heart.

It is the hour
for the tenor
of remembrance
to haunt the sanctuary
in a yearning voice:
                    'KOL NIDREI'

And none will later fear
to lay bare
his transgressions
since all have cause
to repent . . .

As the sermon ascends,
it inquires:
     "What are you?
      What may you become?"
(how many can persist
in vanity against it —
for how long?)

Its eloquence echoes
like the harp strings
at Babylon:
     "Who are you?
      Who might you be?"

The challenge seeps
into the congregation:
Pride capitulates,
for the quest reveals
the intercessor's struggle
which, as the prayerful submit,
is theirs . . .

ONENESS breathes
over the Tabernacle;
the Scrolls stand
like glorious pillars.

Upon the crest of atonement
there vibrates now
The Amen-hush
of purity and peace.

Olive tree